WHEN THE YANKEES COME

FORMER SOUTH CAROLINA SLAVES REMEMBER SHERMANS INVASION

Edited with Introduction by

-PAUL C. GRAHAM

Voices from the Dust, Vol. I

Produced in the Republic of South Carolina by

SHOTWELL PUBLISHING LLC
Post Office Box 2592
Columbia, So. Carolina 29202

www.ShotwellPublishing.com

Cover design: Boo Jackson Designs

ISBN-13: 978-0692630099
ISBN-10: 0692630090

First Edition: February 17, 2016

10 9 8 7 6 5 4 3 2 1

DEDICATION

THIS IS NOT A HISTORY BOOK; it is, rather, a book of personal accounts by those who witnessed history. Its intent is not to interpret the events it portrays, but to let those who were there speak for themselves; to let their voices, as it were, speak to us from the dust—from beyond the grave and through the many, many years that separate us from one another.

It is to these dead that I respectfully dedicate this book.

Society is an open-ended partnership between generations. The dead and the unborn are as much members of society as the living. To dishonour the dead is to reject the relation on which society is built—a relation of obligation between generations. Those who have lost respect for the dead have ceased to be trustees of their inheritance. Inevitably, therefore, they lose their sense of obligation to future generations. The web of obligation shrinks to the present tense.

— Edmund Burke

CONTENTS

INTRODUCTION

ALTHOUGH A NATIVE of Columbia, South Carolina, I never knew. No one ever told me. I may have been vaguely aware that it happened, but I do not recall ever formally breaching the subject. Not at home. Not at school. Not in conversation.

I was told about the stars on the side of the South Carolina Statehouse that marked where Union cannonballs hit. I was told about the cane that was broken-off the statue of George Washington by Yankee soldiers, but I was never told about the fire.

Perhaps they thought that I already knew or should have known, but I didn't. It was not until a friend of mine wrote his senior thesis on the *Burning of Columbia* in the 1990s that I looked into the matter for the first time. I was in my 20s and a graduate student at the University of South Carolina. At the time I really didn't have any interest in the South, the "Civil War," or anything related thereto—I'm not even sure I considered myself to be Southern, at least not without some kind of disclaimer—but I read his thesis nonetheless.

The major source for many of the details in his work came from William Gilmore Simms's *The Sack and Destruction of Columbia, South Carolina* (1865). After reading his thesis, I decided I should read the Simms account as well to get more details on this incredible event. What I read upset me tremendously.

Columbia—*my* city, *my* home—burned to the ground? Wasn't it a surrendered city? Wasn't it occupied entirely by non-combatants—women, children, old men, and servants? Yes, but it was still invaded and destroyed; ruthlessly and without pity.

What was even more shocking than the horrific details of the affair was that this devastation was inflicted by an army of the United States of America. This ran contrary to *everything* I had been taught and, at that time, believed about my country; yet, there it was—theft, vandalism, arson, RAPE, and MURDER—all perpetrated by Union troops; not in some far-away land, but in my own back yard; not against a foreign army, but against my own people, my *family*! They were not people who "deserved it" or "had it coming," they were people I knew to be decent and God fearing. I always knew I had "Confederates in the closet," but I had always considered myself to be a proud American. This, however, shook me to the core. I was not proud after reading this. I was angry.

How could it be that an event of this magnitude was entirely unknown to me? How was it that those who knew or should have known knew little? Said so little? Why were these titbits of information not mentioned in the American History courses I took at college; on a campus located in the heart of the very city where this outrage occurred? Why does Columbia's local newspaper declare every February 17th that "we" still do not know how the city caught on fire or who was responsible for it? WHY?

It seemed to me complete bullshit. Still does.

* * *

ALTHOUGH I REMAINED interested in the details of this event and collected many accounts of Sherman's march across South Carolina, I had never written or edited anything on this topic for publication. It was not until the City of Columbia "commemorated" the sesquicentennial of the *Burning of Columbia* in February 2015 that I was moved to do so.

To be honest, I was not expecting much from the City of Columbia's "commemoration." Their official web site does not even *acknowledge* that there was a war between the years 1861 and 1865, much less that Columbia was destroyed by fire. I thought, however, that *maybe*, just *maybe*, some of these first-hand accounts might find their way out of the dustbins and into the sesquicentennial commemoration.

There were, to be fair, a few decent museum exhibits and— thankfully! —a couple of lectures by some local authors that related many of the less savoury details of this important event, but these were held in libraries and out of the way locations. They were not "headline" events.

It did not take long for me to realize that this "commemoration" was going to be, at least for the most part, a forum on race relations—the evils of slavery, the struggles of the Civil Rights movement of the 1960s, and all the work that is left to be done to achieve the egalitarian dream of the Reverend Dr. Martin Luther

King, Jr.

These, no doubt, are topics of interest and perhaps even importance, but they had *nothing* to do with the *Burning of Columbia*—the actual event being "commemorated."

Sadly, the opportunity to let the dead tell their tales would be lost; the participants would remain in the dark on the details of the burning of Columbia even in the midst of "remembering" it.

* * *

I THOUGHT THAT SINCE the topic of slavery was of such interest to the planners and participants of this commemoration, that it might be interesting to explore the words of former slaves and what they had to say about Sherman's invasion.

I decided to employ a rather unconventional, but extremely interesting and useful resource to accomplish this end: *The Slave Narratives: A Folk History of Slavery in the United States*. (Hereafter, the *Narratives*.)

The *Narratives* were collected by the *Federal Writers' Project* of the *Works Progress Administration*, one of many "New Deal" projects created under President Franklin Delano Roosevelt's administration during the Great Depression in the 1930s. This federally funded project encompassed 17 States and came to comprise over ten thousand typed pages containing over 2000 interviews. The actual work was directed at the state level and is organised by state.

The South Carolina interviews, which occurred 1936-1938, take up four volumes of the collected works. The extracts in this book come exclusively from the South Carolina volumes and, thus, only takes account of the South Carolina experience

While it is true, much has been made of the purported shortcomings of the *Narratives*, I believe a careful review of these narratives, together with other primary source documents (which will be explored in future installments), it is not unreasonable to conclude that these so-called "shortcomings" have more to do with their deviation from the official *Nationalist* or "Yankee" narrative of the events than anything of real substance. There is good reason, at least on the topic at hand, to take these accounts seriously.

While each individual account may be scant and inconclusive in its own right, taken *together*, the *Narratives* present a compelling picture of the event.

A single tile tells us very little about a particular mosaic; however, each one contributes *to* and is necessary *for* the construction of the image. Each account in the *Narratives*, taken on its own—each "tile" as it were—provides us with a rather incomplete picture. Taken together, however, they tell us much.

Of the 285 accounts in the South Carolina Narratives, 114 or 40% of those interviewed have something to say about "when the Yankees come." Of these, 61 (38%) reported theft, 13 (11%) reported vandalism, *i.e.*, destruction of property that did not terminate in arson, 43 (38%) reported arson, and 10 (9%) reported the slaughter of livestock and/or the destruction of foodstuffs, items neither taken nor consumed by troops, nor edible to those left behind.

I have included every relevant account in the four volumes and present them without any further comment below. The order of the interviewees is alphabetical—exactly as they appear in the collection from which I worked.

The language, grammar, and usage of the *Narratives* is left completely intact. I have, however, endeavoured to make each entry as readable as possible, especially for those who are unfamiliar or uncomfortable with dialect, by silently changing words such as "de" to "the," "dem" to "them," "wid" to "with," *et cetera.*

My primary interest being what they said, not how they said it. I have not, however, edited out words that are now considered offensive or "politically incorrect."

The image that emerges when the pieces are assembled is an imposing and terrible one—a desolation of biblical proportion!

Thankfully, there are a few acts of humanity and even kindness by those who wore the blue, and I am most pleased to include them in this otherwise bleak and depressing assemblage of testimonies, but their scarcity in these accounts, I would argue, are a blot on the character and the cause for which they contended. Perhaps you will agree.

Paul C. Graham
Cayce, South Carolina
February 2016

And thou shalt be brought down, and shalt speak out of the ground, and thy speech shall be low out of the dust, and thy voice shall be, as of one that hath a familiar spirit, out of the ground, and thy speech shall whisper out of the dust.

— Isaiah 29:4 (KJV)

THE SLAVE NARRATIVES
VOLUME XIV

SOUTH CAROLINA, PART I

EZRA ADAMS

Near Swansea, Lexington County, SC. Age 83.

There's one thing I does know; the Yankees didn't touch our plantation, when they come through South Carolina. Up in the northern part of the county they sure did destroy most all what folks had.

VICTORIA ADAMS

Columbia, Richland County, SC. Age 90.

Before the Yankees come thru, our peoples had let loose a lot of our horses and the horses strayed over to the Yankee side, and the Yankee men rode the horses back over to our plantation. The

Yankees asked us if we want to be free. I never say I did; I tell them I want to stay with my missus and they went on and let me alone. They destroyed most everything we had except a little vittles; took all the stock and take them with them. They burned all the buildings except the one the master and missus was living in.

FRANCES ANDREWS

Newberry, Newberry County, SC. Age 83.

I married Allen Andrews after the war. He went to the war with his master. He was at Columbia with the Confederate troops when Sherman burnt the place.

PETE ARTHUR

Union, Union County, SC. Age c.85

No ma'am, I never seed Sherman but I seed some of his soldiers. That's the time I run off in the wood and not a soul knowed where I was until the dust had done settled in the big road.

JOSEPHINE BACCHUS

Marion, Marion County, SC. Age 75-80.

Yankees! Oh, I hear folks speak about the Yankees plundering through the country plenty times. Hear about the Yankees going all about stealing white people silver. Say, everywhere they went and found white folks with silver, they would just clean the place up.

CHARLEY BARBER

Near Winnsboro, Fairfield County, SC. Age 81

When the Yankees come they seem to have special vengeance for my white folks. They took everything they could carry off and burnt everything they couldn't carry off.

MILLIE BARBER

Winnsboro, Fairfield County, SC. Age 82.

The Yankees come and burn the gin-house and barns. Open the smokehouse, take the meat, give the slaves some, shoot the chickens, and as the mistress and girls beg so hard, they left without burning the dwelling house.

ANDERSON BATES

Winnsboro, Fairfield County, SC. Age 87.

I was fifteen when the Yankees come thru. They took off everything, horses, mules, cows, sheep, goats, turkeys, geese, and chickens. Hogs? Yes sir, they kill hogs and take off what parts they want and leave other parts bleeding on the yard. When they left, old master have to go up into Union County for rations.

ANNE BELL

Winnsboro, Fairfield County, SC. Age 83.

I was about ten years old when the Yankees come. They was full to the brim with mischief. They took the frocks out the presses and put them on and laugh and carry on powerful. Before they went they took everything. They took the meat and provisions out the smoke-house, and the molasses, sugar, flour, and meal out the house. Killed the pigs and cows, burnt the gin-house and cotton, and took off the livestock, geese, chickens and turkeys.

SAMUEL BOULWARE

Columbia, Richland County, SC. Age 82.

I remembers like yesterday, the Yankees coming along. Master tried to hide the best stuff on the plantation but some of the slaves that helped him hide it, showed the Yankee soldiers just where it was, when they come there. They say: 'Here is the stuff, hid here, because us put it there.' Then the soldiers went straight to the place where the valuables was hid and dug them out and took them, it sure set old master down. Us slaves was sorry that day for master and mistress. They was getting old, and now they had lost all they had, and more than that, they knowed their slaves was set free. The soldiers took all the good horses, fat cattle, chickens, the meat in the smoke house, and then burnt all empty houses. They left the ones that folks lived in. The Yankees appear to me, to be looking for things to eat, more than anything else.

ANDY BRICE

Near Ridgeway, Fairfiled County, SC. Age 81.

I remembers very little about the war, although I was a good size boy when the Yankees come. By instinct, a nigger can make up his mind pretty quick about the creed of white folks, whether they am buckra or whether they am not. Every Yankee I see had the stamp of poor white trash on them. They strutted around, big like fashion, a busting in rooms without knocking, talking free to the white ladies, and familiar to the slave gals, ransacking drawers, and running their bayonets into feather beds, and into the flower beds in the yards.

GEORGE BRIGGS

Union, Union County, SC. Age 88.

When us got to Charleston, us turned around and the bosses fetched us right back to Union through Columbia. Us heard that Sherman was coming, fetching fire along behind him.

ANNE BROOME

Winnsboro, Fairfield County, SC. Age 87.

When the Yankees come, all the young masters was off in the Confederate side. I see them now, galloping to the house, canteen boxes on their hips and the bayonets rattling by their sides. The first thing they ask was: 'You got any wine?' They search the house; make us sing: 'Good Old Time Religion'; put us to running after the chickens and a cooking. When they leave they burnt the gin-house and everything in there. They burn the smoke-house and wind-up with burning the big house.

HENRY BROWN

Charleston, Charleston County, SC. Age 79.

My father, Abram Brown, was the driver or head man at Rose plantation. Dr. Rose thought a heap of him, and during the war he put some of his fine furniture and other things he brought from England in my father's house and told him if the Yankees came to say the things belonged to him. Soon after that the soldiers came. They asked my father who the things belonged to and he said they belonged to him. The soldiers asked him who gave them to him, and he said his master gave them to him. The Yankees told him that they thought he was lying, and if he didn't tell the truth they would kill him, but he wouldn't say anything else so they left him alone and went away.

JOHN C. BROWN

Near Woodward, Fairfield County, SC. Age 86.

The Yankees come and burn the mansion, the gin-house and the mill. They take all the sheep, mules, cows, hogs and even the chickens. Set the slaves free and us niggers have a hard time ever since.

SARA BROWN

Marion, Marion County, SC. Age 85.

I remembers the Yankees come there to my white folks' plantation one day and, child, there was a time on that place. All them niggers was just a kicking up they heels and shouting. I was standing there on the piazza looking at them and I say, 'I don't see why they want to carry on like that for. I been free all the time.' When they get through the Yankees tell them they was free as they Master was and give them so many bushels of corn and so much meat for they own. Some take they pile and go on off and some choose to stay on there with they Missus...

MARGARET BRYANT

Murrells Inlet, Georgetown County, SC. Age Unknown.

Whole gang of Yankee come to the house and didn't do a thing but catch a gang of fowl and gone on. And tell the people to take the house and go in and get what they want. The overseer hear the Doctor whistle to the gate and wave him back. And then the Doctor know the Yankee been there and he gone on to the creek house and get all he gold and thing out the house and gone—Marion until Freedom then he come back. Yankee come in that night. Moon shine like a day. Stay in the Doctor house that night. Morning come, take a gang of fowl and gone on!

SAVILLA BURRELL

Winnsboro, Fairfield County, SC. Age 83.

Us looked for the Yankees on that place like us look now for the Savior and the host of angels at the second coming. They come one day in February. They took everything carryable off the plantation and burnt the big house, stables, barns, gin house and they left the slave houses.

ISAIAH BUTLER

Garnett, Hampton County, SC. Age 79.

I remember when the Yankees come through. I was no more than a lad, nine or ten years old. Bostick had a big gin-house, barn, stables, and such like. And when the soldiers come a goat was up on the platform in front of the door to the loft of the barn. There were some steps leading up there and that goat would walk up them steps same as anybody. The first thing the Yankees do, they shoot that goat. Then day start and tear up everything. All the white folks had refugeed up North, and they didn't do nothing to us niggers.

SOLBERT BUTLER

Scotia, Hampton County, SC. Age 82.

The Yankees kill all the hog. Kill all the cow. Kill all the fowl. Left you nothing to eat. If the colored folk had any chicken, they just had to take that and try to raise them something to eat.

GRANNY CAIN

Newberry, Newberry County, SC. Age 90.

The Yankees went through Maybinton but didn't get over as far as us. Some say they stole cattle and burned gin houses.

THOMAS CAMPBELL

Winnsboro, Fairfield County, SC. Age 82.

Does I remembers the Yankees? Yes sir, I remember when they come. It was cold weather, February, now that I think of it. Oh, the sights of them days. They camp all around up at Mt. Zion College and stable their horses in one of the rooms. They gallop here and yonder and burn the Episcopal Church on Sunday morning. A holy war they called it, but they and Wheeler's men was a holy terror to this part of the world, as naked and hungry as they left it.

SYLVIA CANNON

Florence, Florence County, SC. Age 85.

Us had big rolls of money and then when the Yankees come and change the money, that what made us poor. It let the white people down and let us down too. Left us all to about starve to death.

SILVIA CHISOLM

Estill, Hampton County, SC. Age 88.

I saw them burn down me Master's home, and everything. I remembers that. Old man Joe Bostick was me Master. And I knows the Missus and the Master used to work us. Had the overseer to drive us! Work us until the Yankees come! When Yankee come they had to run! That how the building burn! After they didn't find no one in it, they burn! The Marshall house had a poor white woman in it! That why it didn't burn! My Master's Pineland place at Garnett was burn, too.

REV. TUFF COLEMAN

Newberry, Newberry County, SC. Age 80.

When the Yankees came through at the end of the war, they took all the stock we had. The mistress had a fine horse, its tail touching the ground, and we all cried when it was taken; but we got it back, as some men went after it.

LOUISA COLLIER

Marion, Marion County, SC. Age 78.

I remember one day there come a crowd of peoples there that they tell us children was the Yankees. They come right there through the Colonel yard and when I see them, I was afraid of them. I run and hide under my grandmammy bed. Don't know what they say because

I ain't get close enough to hear nothing what they talk about. The white folks had to hurry and put things in pots and bury them or hide them somewhere when they hear that the Yankees was coming because they scare them Yankees might take they things like they is carry away other folks things. I hear them say they never take nothing from the Colonel but some of he wood.

DINAH CUNNINGHAM

Near Ridgeway, Fairfield County, SC. Age 84.

When the Yankees come, they went through the big house, tore up everything, ripped open the feather beds and cotton mattresses, searching for money and jewels. Then they had us slaves catch the chickens, flung open the smoke-house, take the meat, meal, flour, and put them in a four-horse wagon and went on down to Longtown. Them was scandalous days, boss! I hope never to see the likes of them times with these old eyes again.

LUCY DANIELS

Lurray, Hampton County, SC. Age 78.

My grandmother say the Yankees come to her house and take everything, but she say one little pullet run out in the weeds and hide and the soldiers couldn't find her. She say that pullet lay and hatch and that how they got start off again.

JOHN N. DAVENPORT

Newberry, Newberry County, SC. Age 89.

I remember hearing about the Yankees. When they come through here they camped in town to keep order and peace.

CHARLIE DAVIS

Marion, Marion County, SC. Age 88.

When them Yankees talk about coming around, my Master take all we colored boys and all he fast horses and put them back in the woods to the canebrake to hide them from the Yankees. It been many a year since then, but I recollects that we was sitting there looking for the Yankees to get as any minute. Wasn't obliged to make no noise neither. Oh, we had big chunk of lightwood and cook meat and hoecake and collards right there in the woods. Then my Master take one of them oldest plantation boys to the war with him and ain't nobody never hear tell of him no more. He name Willie. O my Lord, when they hear talk about the Yankees coming, they take all the pots and the kettles and hide them in holes in the fields and they put they silver about some tree so they know where they bury it. Then they hide the meat and the corn to the colored peoples house and when they hear talk of the Yankees going away, they go and get them again. Them Yankees never destroy nothing about there, but they is make my Master give them a cart of corn and a middling of meat. Yes ma'am, I look at them Yankees with me own eyes. They was all dressed up in a blue uniform and they was just as white as you is. Oh, they said a lot of things. Say they was going free the niggers and if it hadn't been for them, we would been slaves until yet. Of course I rather be free than a slave, but we never have so much worries then as people have these days.

HEDDIE DAVIS

Marion, Marion County, SC. Age 72.

Yes ma'am, the Yankees, I hear my daddy talk about when they come through old Master's plantation and everything what they do. Say, there was a old woman that was the cook to the big house and when them Yankees come there that morning, white folks had her down side the cider press just a whipping her. Say, the Yankees took the old woman and dressed her up and hitched up a buggy and made her set up in there. Wouldn't let the white folks touch her no more neither. Oh, the place was just took with them, he say. What they never destroy, they carried off with them. Oh, Lord a mercy, hear talk there was a swarm of them and while some of them was in the house a tearing up, there was a lot of them in the stables takin the horses out. Yes ma'am, some was doing one thing and some another. And Pa tell about they had the most sense he ever did see. Hitched up a cart and kept the path right straight down in the woods and carted the corn up what the white folks been hide down there in the canebrake. Then some went in the garden and dug up a whole lot of dresses and clothes. And there was a lady in the house sick while all this was going on. Oh, they was the worst people there ever was, Pa say. Took all the hams and shoulders out the smokehouse and like I tell you, what they never carried off, they made a scaffold and burned it up. Lord, have mercy, I hopes I ain't going never have to meet no Yankees.

HENRY DAVIS

Winnsboro, Fairfield County, SC. Age 80.

I remember the Yankees coming and searching the house, taking off the cows, mules, horses, and burning the gin-house and cotton. They say that was General Sherman's orders. They was allowed to leave the dwelling house standing, in case of a doctor or preacher. Miss Lizzie had a whole lot of chickens. Her always keep the finest pullets. She make pies and chicken salad out of the oldest hens. That February the Yankees got here, she done save up about fifty pullets that was ready to lay in March. A squad of Yankees make us children catch every one and you know how they went away with them pullets? They tie two on behind, in the rings of the saddle. Then they tie two pullets together and hang them on the saddle pommel, one on each side of the horse's neck. That throw them flanking the horse's withers. I remembers now them galloping off, with them chickens fluttering and hollering whare, whare, whare, whare, whare!

JESSE DAVIS

Winnsboro, Fairfield County, SC. Age c.85.

When the Yankees come thru, they come before the main army. They gallop right up, jump down and say: 'Hold these horses! Open that smoke-house door!' They took what they could carry away. About that time master rode up from a sick call him been attending to. Of course you know him was a doctor. They surround him, take his watch, money, and horse, and ride away. The main army come next day, Saturday morning about 8 o'clock. They spread their tents and stay and camp until Monday morning. When they leave they carry off all the cows, hogs, mules, and horses. Then they have us catch the chickens, got them all, except one old hen that run under the house, and they didn't wait to get her. Master have to go way up to Union County, where him have kin folks, to get something to eat.

LOUISA DAVIS

Winnsboro, Fairfield County, SC. Age 106.

When the Yankees come they took off all they couldn't eat or burn, but don't let's talk about that. Maybe if our folks had beat them and get up into their country our folks would have done just like they did. Who knows?

WALLACE DAVIS

Newberry, Newberry County, SC. Age 88.

The Yankees went through our place and stole cattle... Just after the war the Yankees marched through our place and stole some cattle and run away with them. In some places they burned down the barns and gin houses.

ISABELLA DORROH

Newberry, Newberry County, SC. Age 75.

When the Yankees come through here, they stole everything they could get their hands on. They went in the house and took food and articles. Master put guards around his house to keep them out so they wouldn't steal all the potatoes and flour he had for his slaves.

LAURENCE DOWNING

Newberry, Newberry County, SC. Age 80.

The Yankees went through here and stole all the cattle and all the eats.

WASHINGTON DOZIER

Marion, Marion County, SC. Age. 90.

The Yankees come through there and to my knowing, they behaved very well.

South Carolina, Part 2

MOM RYER EMMANUEL

Claussen, Florence County, SC. Age 78.

Oh, my Lord, when the Yankees come through there, I hear them say it was the Republicans. Mr. Ross had done say that he hear talk that they was coming through and he tell his niggers to hurry and hide all the plantation rations. Yes, ma'am, they dig cellars under the colored people houses and bury what meat and barrels of flour they could and that what they couldn't get under there, they hide it up in the loft. Mr. Ross say, 'Won't none of them damn Yankees get no chance to stick they rotten tooth in my rations.' We say, 'Ma, you got all these rations here and we hungry.' She say, 'No, them ration belong to boss and you children better never bother them neither.' Then when Mr. Ross had see to it that they had fix everything safe, he take to the swamp. That what my mammy say cause he know they wasn't going bother the womens. Lord, when them Yankees ride up to the big house, Miss Ross been scared to open her mouth because the man was in the swamp. No, child, they didn't bother nothing much, but some of the rations they get hold of. Often times, they would come through and kill chickens and butcher a cow up and cook it right there. Would eat all they wanted and Then when they would go to leave, they been call all the little plantation niggers to come there and would give them what was left. Oh, Lord, us was glad to get them vitals, too. Yes, ma'am, all they had left, they would give it to the poor colored people. Us been so glad, us say that us wish they would come back again. Then after they had left us plantation, they would go some other place where there was another crowd of little niggers and would left them a pile of stuff, too. Old Massa, he been stay in the swamp till he hear them Yankees been leave there and Then he come home and would keep sending to the colored people houses to get a little bit of his rations to a time.

LEWIS EVANS

Near Winnsboro, Fairfield County, SC. Age 96.

The Yankees come. First thing they look for was money. They put a pistol right in my forehead and say: 'I got to have your money, where is it?' There was a gal, Caroline, who had some money; they took it away from her. They took the geese, the chickens and all that was worth taking off the place, stripped it. Took all the meat out the smoke-house, corn out the crib, cattle out the pasture, burnt the gin-house and cotton. When they left, they shot some cows and hogs and left them lying right there. There was an awful smell round there for weeks after.

ANN FERGUSON

Estill, Hampton County, SC. Age 74.

My mother was at Old Allendale when the Yankees come through. She was in the kitchen at the time. I was quite small. Around two years old—now how old that make me, Miss? 74? Well, I knows I is getting along. I remember them talking about it all. They searched the house, and take out what they want, Then set the house afire. Ma, she run out then and whoop and holler. The lady of the house was there, but the Master had went off.

JOHN FRANKLIN

Columbia, Richland County, SC. Age 84.

After we walk along the Broad River road, what seem to us for a quarter of a mile, we see four or five old men standing on the left side of the road waving a white flag. We walks out in the woods on the right side opposite and watches. Soon we see what seem like a thousand men on horses coming briskly along. The men keep waving the white flag. After many had passed, one big bearded man rein up his horse and speak with the men waving the white flag. They tell the soldier there am no 'Rebel soldier' in Columbia and the blue-clad army am welcome; begging them to treat the old folks, women and children, well. The Yankee soldier set straight and solemn on his horse, and when the old men finish and hand him a paper, he salute and tell them, 'Your message will be laid before General Sherman'.

All this time the ground am shaking from the roar of big guns across the river. Ben and me run thru the woods to our foot log and see thousands still coming into Columbia, all along. We get afraid and stayed in the woods until we get out of sight of the soldiers. But we ain't got far over the top of the hill until we come face to face with more men on horses. One of the men, who seem to be the leader, stop his horse and ask us boys some questions. We answer as best we can, when he grin at us and pull out some money and give us a nickel a piece.

We travel on toward Chapin and meet our mammies and many other people, some them white. They all seem scared and my mammy and Ben's mammy and us, turns up the river and camps on the hill, for the night, in the woods. We never sleep much, for it was almost as light as day, and the smell of smoke was terrible. We could see people running in certain parts of Columbia, sometimes. Next morning we look over the city from the bluff and only a few houses was standing and hundreds of tumble-down chimneys and the whole town was still smoking. I dreams yet about that awful time, but I thank God that he has permitted me to live long enough to see the city rebuilt and it stretching far over the area where we hid in the trees.

ADELE FROST

Near Columbia, Richland County, SC. Age 93.

The Yankees take three nights to march through I was afraid of them and climb into a tree. One call me down and say, "I am your friend'". He give me a piece of money and I wasn't afraid no more.

AMOS GADSDEN

Charleston, Charleston County, SC. Age 88.

Sherman set fire everywhere he went—didn't do much fighting, just wanted to destroy as he went.

LUCY GALLMAN

Newberry, Newberry County, SC. Age 80.

When the Yankees went through their soldiers stole everything, all horses and supplies. The soldiers stopped at places, and like the soldiers who come home foot-sore, they was lousy and dirty... The Yankee soldiers would take our rations at our gates and eat them up. They would blow bugles at we children and beat drums. Our old Missus would take victuals to them.

GRACIE GIBSON

Winnsboro, Fairfield County, SC. Age 86.

I remember Wheeler's men come to our house first, before the Yankees. They took things just like the Yankees did that come later. Master John was a Captain, off fighting for Confederates but that didn't stop Wheeler's men from takin' things they wanted, no sir! They took what they wanted. Wasn't long after then that the Yankees come and took all they could and burnt what they couldn't carry off with them.

JOHN GLOVER

Timmonsville, Florence County, SC. Age 77.

I can tell you all about when them Yankees come through there. Some was on black horses, some on red horses, and some on white horses. The one that on black horse wear black, the one on white horse wear white, and the one on the red horse wear red. The horses had sense enough to double up when that man hollo from the top of them. They was wearing soldier clothes and they come up to you house and set place on fire, kill cow or anything they want to. They burn up Carson house and stay there until next day. They talk to my mamma cause our house the next one to the white folk's house. The white folks done been gone. They ask her where they hide they money and she know they hide it to Stafford Hill, six miles from the house, but she didn't tell them. Don' know yet what became of the money, but them Yankees loaded an old chest on the wagon and took all the slaves that wanted to run away with them and left there.

ELLEN GODFREY

Conway, Horry County, SC. Age 99.

I been a weaver when the Yankee come. I been on the loom to Marlboro district. A man place they call Doctor Major Drake. Got a son name Cap and Pet. Oh, Jesus, been here too long! In my ninety-nine now. Come seven of October been a hundred. Three flat carry two hundred 'o people and all they things. We hide from Yankee but Yankee come and get we. Ask where Master. (Master in swamp!) I in buckra house. I say, 'Them gone! Gone to beach.' Say, 'Tell them to be in Georgetown to bow unto the flag.'

ELIJAH GREEN

Charleston, Charleston County, SC. Age c.94.

When Sherman was coming through Columbia, he fired and a shell lodged in the South-Eastern of the State House which was forbidden to be fixed. He was coming down Main Street when that happens.

ADELINE GREY

Lurray, Hampton County, SC. Age 82.

I remember when the Yankees come through. I was right to the old boss' place. It was on the river side. Miss Jane Warner, she was the missus. The place here now—where all the children raise. Mr. Rhodes got a turpentine still there now—just after you pass the house. They burn the gin house, the shop, the buggy house, the turkey house and the fowl house. Start to set the corn house afire, but my Ma say: 'Please sir, don't burn the corn house. Give it to me and my children.' So they put the fire out. I member when they started to break down the smokehouse door, and old Missus come out and say: 'Please don't break the door open, I got the key.' So they quit. I remember when they shoot down the hog. I remember when they shoot the two geese in the yard. They choked my Ma. They went to her and they say; 'Where is all the white people gold and silver?' My Ma say she don't know. 'You does know!' they say, and choke her till she couldn't talk. They went into the company room where the old Miss was staying and start tearing up the bed. Then the captain come and the old Miss say to him: 'Please don't let them tear up my bed,' and the captain went in there and tell them 'Come out!'.

The old Miss wasn't scared. But the young Miss May was sure scared. She was courting at the time. She went off and shut herself up in a room. The old Miss ask the captain: 'Please go in and talk to the Miss, she so scared'. So he went in and soon he bring her out. We children wasn't scared. But my brother run under the house. The soldiers went under there a-poking the bayonets into the ground to try to find where the silver buried, and they ran across him. 'What you doing under here?' they say. 'I's just running the chickens out, sir,' he say. 'Well, you can go on out,' they say. 'We ain't going to hurt you.'

'I remember when they kill the hog and cook them. Cook on the fire where the little shop been. Cook them and eat them. Why didn't they cook them on the stove in the house? Didn't have no stoves. Just had to cook on the fireplace. Had an oven to fit in the fireplace. I remember when my Ma saw the Yankees coming that morning she grab the sweet potatoes that been in that oven and throw them in the barrel of feathers that stayed by the kitchen fireplace. Just a barrel to hold chicken feathers when you pick them. That's all we had to eat that day. Them Yankees put the meat in the sack and go on off. It was late then, about dusk. I remember how the Missus bring us all around the fire. It was dark then. 'Well children,' she say, 'I is sorry to tell you, but the Yankees has carry off your Ma. I don't know if you'll ever see her any more.' Then we children all start crying. We still a sitting there when my Ma come back. She say she slip behind, and slip behind, slip behind, and when she come to a little pine thicket by the side of the road, she dart into it, drop the sack of meat they had her carrying, and start out for home. When we had all make over her, we say to her then: 'Well why didn't you bring the sack of meat along with you?'

They took the top off old Master John carriage, put meat in it, and made him pull it same as a horse. Carry him way down to Lawtonville, had to pull it through the branch and all. Got the rock-a-way back though—and the old man. I remember that well. Had to mend up the old rock-a-way. And it made the old man sick. He keep on sick, sick, until he died. I remember how he'd say: 'Don't you all worry'. And he'd go out in the orchard. They'd say: 'Don't bother him! Just let him be! He want to pray!' After a while he died and they buried him. His name was John Stafford. They Master wasn't there. I guess he was off to the war.

...Ole Miss had give my Ma a good moss mattress. But the Yankees had carry that off. Rip it up, throw out the moss, and put meat in it. Fill it full of meat. I remember she had a red striped shawl. One of the Yankee take that and start to put in under his saddle for a saddle cloth. My brother go up to him and say: 'Please sir, don't carry my Ma's shawl. That the only one she got.' So he give it back to him. To keep warm at night, they had to make there pallet down by the fire; when all wood burn out, put on another piece. Didn't have nothing on the bed to sleep on.

FANNIE GRIFFIN

Columbia, Richland County, SC. Age 94.

The worst time we ever had was when the Yankee men come thru. We had heard they was coming and the missus tell us to put on a big pot of peas to cook, so we put some white peas in a big pot and put a whole ham in it, so that we'd have plenty for the Yankees to eat. Then when they come, they kicked the pot over and the peas went one way and the ham another. The Yankees destroyed almost everything we had. They come in the house and told the missus to give them her money and jewels. She started crying and told them she ain't got no money or jewels, excepting the ring she had on her finger. They got awfully mad and started destroying everything. They took the cows and horses, burned the gin, the barn, and all the houses except the one master and missus was living in. They didn't leave us a thing except some big hominy and two banks of sweet potatoes. We chipped up some sweet potatoes and dried them in the sun, then we parched them and ground them up and that's all we had to use for coffee. It taste pretty good too. For a good while we just live on hominy and coffee.

SUSAN HAMILTON

Charleston, Charleston County, SC. Age 101.

When the war began we was taken to Aiken, South Carolina where we stay until the Yankees come through. We could see balls sailing through the air when Sherman was coming. Bombs hit trees in our yard.

REV. THOMAS HARPE

Newberry, Newberry County, SC. Age 84.

The Yankees marched through our place, stole cattle, and meat. We went behind them and picked up lots that they dropped when they left.

ABE HARRIS

Near Winnsboro, Fairfield County, SC. Age 74.

My old master, Tom, live up until the Civil War and although he couldn't walk, he equipped and pay a man to go in his place. When Sherman's men come to the house, he was in bed with a dislocated hip. They thought he was shamming, playing opossum, so to speak. One of the raiders, a Yankee, come with a lighted torch and say: 'Unless you give me the silver, the gold, and the money, I'll burn you alive.' Him reply: 'I haven't many more years to live. Burn and be damned!' The Yankee was surprised at his bravery, ordered father to take the torch from under the bed and say: 'You about the bravest man I ever see in South Carolina.

ELIZA HASTY

Near Blackstock, Chester/Fairfield Counties, SC. Age. 85.

The Yankees come. They took notice of me! They was a bad lot that disgrace Mr. Lincoln that sent them here. They insult women both white and black, but the Lord was mindful of his own.

JIM HENRY

Near Winnsboro, Fairfield County, SC. Age 77.

I just can remember the Yankees. Don't remember that they was so bad. You know they say even the devil ain't as black as he is painted. The Yankees did take off all the mules, cows, hogs, and sheep, and ransack the smoke-house, but they never burnt a thing at our place. Folks wonder at that. Some say it was because General Bratton was a high degree Mason.

LUCRETIA HEYWARD

Beaufort, Beaufort County, SC. Age 96.

When Yankee been come the Blunts leave Beaufort, and I walk out house and go back to Parris Island. The Yankee tell we to go and Buckra corn house and get what we want for eat.

MARIAH HEYWOOD

Murrells Inlet, Georgetown County, SC. Age 82.

You could hear them over there slamming and banging. The Yankee tear up the Dr. Flagg house but they didn't come Sunnyside. Bright day too! Old man Thomas Stuart lead them to Hermitage. Had team they take from Mr. Betts and team they take from Dr. Arthur to Woodland... Flat going from Midway to Cheraw. Best rice on flat. Kill chicken. Gone to protect from Yankees—to hide! When they come (to Cheraw). Sherman coming from MONDAY till SATURDAY! Come on RAIL! Said it was a shocking sight! When Sherman army enter Cheraw, town full of soldiers. Take way from white people and give horses colored people! Didn't kill none the horses. (On Sunnyside on Waccamaw) Cheraw Yankee kill horses!

JERRY HILL

Spartanburg, Spartanburg County, SC. Age c.85.

When the Yankee soldiers came my master had to hide out for a while, as he had gotten into some trouble with them at Union. They would search the house occasionally and then go into the woods looking for him. One day the soldiers caught him down on the branch and killed him. As the Yankee soldiers would come to the plantation, they would leave their worn-out horses and take our good ones. They also stole meat, hams, sugar etc.; but they were pretty quiet most of the time. One of our neighbors caught a Yankee stealing his horse and killed him right there. His name was Bill Isom.

All his family is now dead. The soldiers would slip around and steal a good horse and ride it off. We would never see that horse again.

BEN HORRY

Murrells Inlet, Georgetown County, SC. Age 87.

When they think Yankee coming you take to Sandhole Creek for hide. Mr. Carmichael sent by the state. Go to Brookgreen, Longwood, Watsaw. Tell everything surrender. Go to any located place. He's a General... Time of the war the colored people hear about Yankee. Not a one ever understand to run way and go to Yankee boat from WE plantation. These Yankee people was walking about on the beach. And while they come in to the hill, the Reb have a battery to Laurel Hill and they cut off them Yankee from the ocean. These they cut off they carry them to Brookgreen barn. Hang one colored man and one white man to Oaks Seashore. White man must of be sergeant or big Captain... Yankee come here and butt us colored people. I remember we young ones just could tote up them gold pitcher and bury them in the garden. Not far from the flowers tank. Tank have on them a woman head (Flowers' tank was a fountain). All the master fine thing way down there bury! The Ward didn't loss nothing. They move us out the plantation. Col. Ward took them in a flat to Marlboro.

MARGARET HUGHES

Columbia, Richland County, SC. Age 82.

Well little missy, I done told you just about all I remembers except about the Yankees. When I used to hear the older niggers talking about the Yankees coming, I was scared, because I thought it was some kind of animal they was talking about. My old aunty was glad to hear about the Yankees coming. She just sit and talk about what a good time we was going to have after the Yankees come. She'd say; 'Child we going to have such a good time a sitting at the white folks table, a eating off the white folks table, and a rocking in the big rocking chair. Something awful happen to one of the slaves though, when the Yankees did come. One of the young gals tell the Yankees where the missus had her silver, money and jewelry hid, and they got it all. What you think happened to the poor gal? She'd done wrong I know, but I hated to see her suffer so awful for it. After the Yankees had gone, the missus and master had the poor gal hung until she die. It was something awful to see. The Yankees took everything we had except a little food, hardly enough to keep us alive.

HESTER HUNTER

Marion, Marion County, SC. Age 85.

Remember the first time them Yankees come there, I was sitting down in the chimney corner and my mammy was giving me my breakfast. Remember I been sitting there with my milk and my bowl of hominy and I hear my old grandmammy come a running in from out the yard and say all the sky was blue as indigo with the Yankees coming right there over the hill then. Say she see more Yankees than could ever cover up all the premises about there. Then I hear my Missus scream and come a running with a lapful of silver and tell my grandmammy to hurry and sew that up in the feather bed cause them Yankees was mighty apt to destroy all they valuables. Old Missus tell all the colored people to get away, get away and take care of themselves and tell we children to get back to the chimney corner cause she couldn't protect us no ways no longer. Yes, honey, I was a little child sitting there in that chimney corner listening to all that scampering about and I remember that day just as good as it had been this day right here. Oh, my God, them Yankees never bring nothing but trouble and destructiveness when they come here, child. I remember I hear tell that my old stepfather been gone to the mill to grind some corn and when he was coming down the road, two big Yankees jump out the bushes side the road and tell him stop there. He say they tell him if he want to save his neck, he better get off that ox right then and get away from there. He say he been so scared he make for the woods fast as he could get there and tell that he lay down with knots under his head many a night fore he would venture to come out from that woods. Never hear tell of his ox and corn no more neither.

SOUTH CAROLINA, PART 3

ADELINE JACKSON

Winnsboro, Fairfield County, SC. Age 88.

The Yankees that I remembers was not gentlefolks. They stole everything they could take and the meanest thing I ever see was shoats they half killed, cut off the hams, and left the other parts quivering on the ground.

FRED JAMES

Newberry, Newberry County, SC. Age 81.

We heard the Yankees marching before they got there, but they come from the other side of the house, facing south towards Caldwells, and we didn't see them marching in. They stopped at our house and looked around and asked if master was at home. We told him that he wasn't there. We was eating apples, and they asked us where we got them. We told them that we got the apples on the place, and they asked us for some. We give them some apples; Then they left. Master had carried his fine stock about a mile off in the woods so the soldiers couldn't find them; but we didn't tell the soldiers.

HENRY D. JENKINS

Winnsboro, Fairfield County, SC. Age 87.

When the Yankees come, what they do? They did them things they ought not to have done and they left undone the things they ought to have done. Yes, that just about tells it. One thing you might like to hear. Mistress got all the money, the silver, the gold and the jewels, and got the well digger to hide them in the bottom of the well. Them Yankees smart. When they got there, they asked for the very things at the bottom of the well. Mistress wouldn't tell. They held a court of inquiry in the yard; called slaves up, one by one, good many. Must have been a Judas amongst us. Soon a Yankee was let down in the well, and all that money, silver, gold, jewelry, watches, rings, brooches, knives and forks, butter-dishes, waters, goblets, and cups was took and carried away by an army that seemed more concerned about stealing, than they was about the Holy War for the liberation of the poor African slave people. They took off all the horses, sheeps, cows, chickens, and geese, took the seine and the fishes they caught, corn in crib, meat in smoke house, and everything. Master General Sherman said war was hell. It sure was. Maybe it was hell for some of them Yankees when they come to die and give account of the deeds they done in Sumter and Richland Counties.

MARIA JENKINS

Charleston, Charleston County, SC. Age c.90.

When the Yankee come I old enough for mind children, and take them to the field.

ADELINE HALL JOHNSON

Near Winnsboro, Fairfield County, SC. Age 93.

When the Yankees come, they was struck dumb with the way master acted. They took things, with a beg your pardon kind of way, but they never burnt a single thing, and went off with their tails betwixt their legs, kind of ashamed like.

REV. JAMES H. JOHNSON

Columbia, Richland County, SC. Age 82.

I was nearly ten years old, when the army of General Sherman came to Camden. I talked to some of the soldiers, soon after they arrived.

JIMMIE JOHNSON

Spartanburg, Spartanburg County, SC. Age 90.

When the Yankee soldiers come to Spartanburg it scared me. They kept telling me that they were not going to hurt me, but I got a pile of brick-bats and put them under the house. I told Missus I wasn't going to let any of the soldiers hurt her. The Yankee soldiers did not bother me. They came all around our house, but every one of them was quiet and orderly. They took some of Missus' sugar and hams, but did not kill any of the chickens. I told them not to take the sugar, but they took it and the hams anyhow.

MARY JOHNSON

Newberry, Newberry County, SC. Age 85.

Yes, the Yankees was bad. They burnt everything in their way, and stole cattle; but they didn't come near our place.

MARTHA KELLY

Marion, Marion County, SC. Age 70-75.

I hear talk of them Yankees plenty times, but I don' know much to speak about them. Couldn't tell the first word about them. I this kind of person, I don' pay much mind to nothing like that. They was white people, I think.

MARY JANE KELLEY

Newberry, Newberry County, SC. Age 85.

I remember when the Yankees come through after the war. They stole everything and burned up everything they couldn't steal.

GABE LANCE

Murrells Inlet, Georgetown County, SC. Age 77.

I could remember when the Yankee boats come to Montarena—gunboats. About ten o'clock in the morning. Soldier all muster out and scatter all over the island. You know that causeway? Gone over that two by two, gun on shoulder glisten against the sun! Blue-coats, blue pants, hat all blue. Come back to landing about five o'clock. Have hog, geese, duck! Broke in barn. Stole rations from poor people. My Grandfather the Driver—slave Driver. Name Nelson. Master—Frank Harriott. Master gone in swamp. Hid in woods. My Grandfather take old Miss Sally—Miss Sally Harriott—count she couldn't walk with rheumatism—Grandfather took old Miss Sally on he back to hid them in the woods where Master. Yankee stay but the one day. Ravage all over us island. All goat, hog, chicken, duck, geese—all the animal but the cow been take on the Yankee gun boat. They broke in Master big rice barn and share all that out to the colored folks. Some my people run away from Sandy Island. Go Oaks sea-shore and Magnolia Beach and take row-boat and gone out and join with the Yankee. Them crowd never didn't come back.

BEN LEITNER

Winnsboro, Fairfield County, SC. Age 85.

When the Yankees come, they ransack the house for silver and gold. They burn the house and gin-house; carry off mules, horses, and cows. They took the chickens, load all the provisions, put them in a four-horse wagon, and leave us and the white folks cold and hungry. It was cold winter time then too.

MARY ANN LIPSCOMB

Gaffney, Cherokee County, SC. Age Unknown.

When we heard that the Yankees were coming, we had the Negroes to hide all the horses but two, and to hide the cows and turn the hogs loose to ramble in the woods. When the Yankees rode up to the yard and got off their horses, we could easily tell they had been drinking. We told them that our horses were in the stable and that the Negroes had fled in terror, which was true. They ate up everything they could find and ransacked the closets and pantry. They then caught the chickens, took the two horses in the stable and went away. The darkies came back with the cows and horses, and we got settled for the night. About nine o'clock, the Yankees came unexpectedly and took all the horses and cows. They killed the cows, and made our darkies help them to butcher them and barbecue them. The Yankees soon ate everything up and left with our horses. My grandmother, Agnes Wood, gave my mother, Elizabeth Wilkins, a beautiful young mare. The Yankee who took that mare, turned over a pot of fresh soap when my mother asked him not to take the mare. Our cook, Matilda, had the soap ready to cut in the pot, so we saved some of it.

GABLE LOCKLIER

Gourdin, Williamsburg County, SC. Age 86.

I remembers the Yankees come to the house one day. The white folks had a bull dog tied in the smoke house and one Yankee hold the gun on the dog and another take the meat out the house. Then they come out and set table and eat. Dog didn't try to bite them because dog know when to bite. Somebody ask them to have some rice and they say, 'I would cut my throat before I eat that thing.

NELLIE LOYD

Newberry, Newberry County, SC. Age c.91.

The Yankees come through our section, and Master hid his meat and things in deep holes that he dug in the cemetery. He built a fence around the cemetery. The Yankees took good horses and left poor ones. They made niggers cook for them all night.

AMIE LUMPKIN

Columbia, Richland County, SC. Age 88.

I was sixteen when Sherman's army come through Fairfield County. I see them riding by for hours, some of them laughing and many of them has big balls in their hands, which they throw against the house and it explode and burn the house.

I have always suspected that am just the way they set the houses when Columbia was burned in a single night. Some of the houses in

Fairfield was burned, some in Winnsboro, and others in the country, but Columbia was the only place that was wiped out. As the army pass, we all stand by the side of the road and cry and ask them not to burn our white folks' house, and they didn't.

GEORGE MCALILLEY

Winnsboro, Fairfield County, SC. Age 84.

Does I recollect the Yankees? I sure does. They burnt the gin-house and school house. Took the mules, horses, chickens, and eggs. Master was sharp enough to bury the meat in the woods, along with other things they didn't get. They set the house afire at the last, and rode off. Us put the fire out and save the mansion for Maser John.

ED MCCROREY

Winnsboro, Fairfield County, SC. Age 82.

The Yankees never burn up the house. It catch a fire from a spark out the chimney of the house that Master Troy was habituating then. Yes sir, Yankees took all they could carry way, but didn't touch the house. Master Troy kept a bar and lots of poor white trash continually around there smoking. Suspect some of them no account folks caused the fire.

BILL MCNEIL

Ridgeway, Fairfield County, SC. Age 82.

See lots of the Yankees and their doings in war time. They just ride high, burn and take off everything from us, like they did everywhere else.

ANDY MARION

Winnsboro, Fairfield County, SC. Age 92.

What did the Yankees do when they come? They tied me up by my two thumbs, try to make me tell where I hided the money and gold watch and silver, but I swore I didn't know. Did I hide it? Yes, so good it was two years before I could find it again. I put everything in a keg, went into the woods, spaded the dirt by a pine stump, put the keg in, covered it up with leaves and left it.

LUCINDA MILLER (*VIA INTERVIEWER* F.S. DuPRE)

Spartanburg, Spartanburg County, SC. Age c.82.

When asked how the Yankee soldiers behaved when they came by the farm, she said, "a whole passel of them came by the house one day. They asked the Missus if she had any white bread and some honey." Upon being told that she didn't have any of either, they asked for water. Aunt Lucinda was told to bring them a bucket. She drew the water from the well and, after filling it, she placed it on her head to carry it. The captain of the soldiers told her he could not drink the water from the bucket on her head, so made her place it on a stand. Then after the captain drank, the rest did also. They then came on into the yard and went to the stable, took a mule and rode it off, without saying anything. The missus had heard what the soldiers would do when they came to a farm, so all the valuables had been hidden. The horses were driven way back into the woods, the food stuff and clothing was hidden about the place. She said her mother was a good weaver and used to make lots of good clothes and quilts, but all this was put into a hole and covered up with dirt to keep the soldiers from taking it. Aunt Lucinda said the soldiers did not tarry there long after looking about for horses and such, and soon left. The only thing they got was the mule that was in the stable.

CURETON MILLING

Near Winnsboro, Fairfield County, SC. Age 80.

What about the Yankees? Two come first, and rode up to the kitchen, rode right up to the steps and say: 'Where the silver? Where the gold rings and jewelry you got hid for the white folks? Tell us or us will beat you worse than you ever get beat from the lash of the patrollers.' They was as good as they words; they gets down and grab us and make us tell all us know. Where old master? He done burnt the wind in his buggy with the very things the Yankees asked for and refugeed somewhere away, sir.

SALLIE PAUL

Marion, Marion County, SC. Age 79.

I don' know nothing about the Yankees only I see them come through there the day we was freed, but wasn't no great heap of them come. Of course they was passing through that country all during the war and come to the colored people's house and get something to eat. Yes, ma'am, colored people feed them and give them something to travel on. It just like this, the Yankees would give the colored people they good clothes and take they rags. You see, they was deserting. Was running away and getting back home. I don' know whether if the white folks know about they there or not, but I know one thing, Master didn't see them. Yankees didn't do no harm nowhere in that country to nobody, white nor colored. Never hear tell of that, but white people was scared of the Yankees as they was of a rattlesnake.

AMY PERRY

Charleston, Charleston County, SC. Age 82.

I remembers when the Yankee come thru, and Wheeler army come after them. Those been dreadful times. The Yankees massacred the people, and burn their houses, and stole the meat and everything they could find. The white folks have to live wherever they can, and they didn't have enough to eat. I know whole families live on one goose a week, cook in greens. Sometimes they have pumpkin and corn, red corn at that. Times was hard, hard. The colored people don't have nothing to eat neither.

HENRY PRISTELL

Estill, Hampton County, SC. Age 83.

When the Yankees come, at first sight of them they was string right along as far back as Luray. And string out crossways all over everywhere. They was just as thick together as the panels in this fence. They was thousands of them! It was in the afternoon, and they was over everywhere—over the woods, over the fields, and through the swamps, thick as them weeds out there! They didn't leave anything! They burn the fences down, shoot the cows, the hogs, the turkeys and ducks and geese, the chickens and everything. They didn't stay no time—didn't spend the night—just pass through. I see some of them set a fence afire and stop there and cook. There was rail fences of fat pinewood in them days. For the plantation use, they didn't burn none of the colored folks' houses nor the old boss' house. And as for anybody being injured when they pass through I didn't see none of that. I must speak the truth, ma'am I didn't see anything out of the way. Just burn things and take things to eat. There was Mr. Thomas' place, and Mr. David Horton's place, Then Mr. Wallace' place. They didn't burn any of them.

JUNIUS QUATTLEBAUM

New Brooklyn, Lexington County, SC. Age 84.

Yes, sir, I remembers, like yesterday, when Columbia was burned by the Yankees in 1865. All that happened in the month of February, I thinks. Some of the niggers on the plantation said they seen the smoke from that big fire, but I has my doubts about the truth of that.

SOUTH CAROLINA, PART 4

SAM RAWLS

Newberry, Newberry County, SC. Age 84.

When the Yankees come through burning, killing and stealing stock, I was in master's yard. They come up where the boss was standing, told him there was going to be a battle, grabbed him and hit him. They burned his house, stole the stock, and one Yankee stuck his sword to my breast and said for me to come with him or he would kill me. Of course I went along. They took me as far as Broad River, on the other side of Chapin; then turned me loose and told me to run fast or they would shoot me. I went fast and found my way back home by watching the sun. They told me to not go back to that old man.

JESSE RICE

Gaffney, Cherokee County, SC. Age 80.

You know that I does remember when that Sherman man went through here with them awful mens he had. They allowed that they was going to Charlotte to get back to Columbia. I never is heard of such before or since. We lived at old man Jerry Moss's in Yorkville, way back then. Yes sir, everyone said Yorkville, then, but they ain't never called Gaffney like that. Stories goes round about Sherman shooting folks. Some say that he shot a big rock off in the State House in Columbia. My Ma and my Pa, Henry and Charity Rice, hid me with them when Sherman come along. Us never seed him, Lord God no, us never wanted to see him...

So them Yankees went on somewhere, I never knowed where, and everything around Yorkville was powerful relieved. Then the Confederate soldiers started coming across Broad River. Before they got home, word had done got around that our folks had surrendered; but them Yankees never fought us out—they starved us out. If things had been equal us would a-been fighting them until this day, that us sure would. I can still see them soldiers of ours coming across Broad River, all dirty, filthy, and lousy. They was most starved, and so poor and lanky. And their horses was in the same fix. Men and horses had knowed plenty until that Sherman come along, but most of them never knowed plenty no more. The men got over it better than the horses. Women folks cared for the men.

MAMIE RILEY

Estill, Hampton County, SC. Age c.80.

When the Yankees come through Mr. Solomon's' place I was right there. We was at our house in the street. I see it all. My ma tell me to run; but I ain't think they'd hurt me. I see them come down the street—all of them on horses. Oh, they was a heap of them! I couldn't count them. My daddy run to the woods—he and the other men.

They ran right to the graveyard. Too much a bush been there. You couldn't see them. Stay in the woods three days. They went to my daddy's house and take all. My daddy ran. My mother and my older sister was there. My ma grab a quilt off the bed and cover herself all over with it—head and all. And set in a chair there by the fire. She tell us to get in the bed—but I ain't get in. And she yell out when she hear them coming: 'There's the fever in here!' Six of them come to the door; but they say they ain't going in—they'll catch the fever. Then some more come along. They say they going in. They ain't going to take no fever. Fill two sack of potatoes. White man ask to search all trunk. They take two of me Ma's good dresses out. Say to wrap potatoes in. I start to crying then, and they say, 'Well, get us some sacks then.' I knowed where some sacks was. I get them the sacks. They do them right. They bid them goodbye, and asked them where the man was. They give me eleven or twelve dollars. I was little and ain't know. My mother never give it to me.

ISOM ROBERTS

Columbia, Richland County, SC. Age. 80.

I was a very small boy when the Civil War was going on. It seems like I knows all about Sherman's army coming through this State, a burning Columbia and destroying and taking away everything what folks had. I has heard so much about slavery and all them times, from my mammy and daddy, that it appears to me that I experienced it all. I suspects knowing about things is just about as good and true as seeing them. Don't you?

ALEXANDER ROBERTSON

Near White Oak, Marion County, SC. Age 84.

What the Yankees do when they come? Let other people tell that, but seem like they lay the whole town in ashes, except the college and our house close to it, that they use for the officers while they was in [Winns]Boro. Why they hear something about the Davis name teaching the St. John Episcopal Church and they march around there, one cold February Sunday morning, set it afire, and burn it up. Mother and me went to the plantation and stayed there until they left.

CHARLIE ROBINSON

Near Winnsboro, Fairfield County, SC. Age 87.

The Yankees made a clean sweep of everything, horses, mules, cows, hogs, meat and molasses. Got so mad when they couldn't find any salt, they burn up everything. Pull Master Joe's beard, just because him name Beard. The one that do that was just a smart aleck and the captain of the crowd shame him and make him slink away, out the house.

AL ROSBORO

Near Winnsboro, Fairfield County, SC. Age 90.

Yankees come and burn up everything him have.

REUBEN ROSBOROUGH

Ridgeway, Fairfield County, SC. Age 82.

Indeed I recollects about the Yankees. They come and ask my pappy, the foreman, where was the mules and horses hid out? Pappy say he don't know, he didn't carry them off. They find out a boy that knowed; make him tell, and they went and got the mules and horses. They took everything and left.

ELIZA SCANTLING

Scotia, Hampton County, SC. Age 87.

On a Monday morning a colored man come along and tell Miss Anna the Yankees had took Waynesboro. We all went to see it. The fire had left the place clean. Could pick up a pin behind it. Other than that I see nothing. I never see no house burn down. I never hear no gun fire. I just see the uniform, and see them kill the hog and sling them across the saddle. Then when we come back to Robertville, we see the destruction left behind.

NINA SCOTT (*via* INTERVIEWER F.S. DuPre)

Spartanburg, Spartanburg County, SC. Age Unknown.

"When the 'raid' came on, people were hiding things all about their places." She referred to the Yankee soldiers who came to Spartanburg after the close of the Civil War. "My mother hid the turkeys and told me where she had hidden them." Dr. Shipp came up to Nina one day and asked her where the turkeys were hidden. She told him they were hidden behind a clump of small trees, and pointed them out to him. "Well," he said, "tell your mother to go and hide them somewhere else and not to tell you about it. You would tell the Yankees just where those turkeys were hidden."

ALFRED SLIGH

Columbia, Richland County, SC. Age 100.

We work on, until Sherman come and burn and slash his way through the state in the spring of 1865.

DAN SMITH

Winnsboro, Fairfield County, SC. Age 75.

When the Yankees come, mammy hide us children under her bed 'traption. They act mighty nice to her, so she say.

JANE SMITH (*VIA* INTERVIEWER F.S. DuPRE)

Spartanburg, Spartanburg County, SC. Age 80.

Aunt Jane said that when the Yankee soldiers came to the house, they were just as thick as the "fingers on her hands." She held up her hands for inspection to illustrate how thick the soldiers stood in the ranks. She said they did not take anything, but that they crawled under the house to get the hen eggs. One soldier, she said, came to the house and asked if there were any horses on the farm. A colored woman told him that there were no horses on the place, but just at that time, one of the horses in a nearby stable neighed, and the soldier threatened the woman's life for lying to him. She says she doesn't remember whether the soldier took the horses but thinks that he did.

JESSIE SPARROW

Marion, Marion County, SC. Age 83.

I recollects I see them Yankees when they come through my Master plantation and took his best carriage horse. Had two of them big black carriage horses that was match horses and them Yankees carry one of them away with them. I hear them say the white folks would bury they silver and money in pots and barrels to hide them from the Yankees. Oh, them fiddling Yankees asked nobody nothing. Just go in the house and take that what they wanted. Go right in the house and plunder round and take the peoples best things. Wouldn't take no common things. Wasn't right, but they done it.

ROSA STARKE

Near Winnsboro, Fairfield County, SC. Age 83.

The Yankees come set all the cotton and the gin-house afire. Load up all the meat; take some of the sugar and shovel some over the yard; take all the wine, rum, and liquor; gut the house of all the silver and valuables, set it afire, and leave one thousand niggers cold and hungry, and our white folks in a misery they never has got over to the third generation of them. Some of them is the poorest white folks in this State today. I weeps when I sees them so poor, but they is respectable yet, thank God.

JOSEPHINE STEWART

Blackstock, Chester/Fairfield, SC. Age 85.

The Yankees burned and stole everything on the place. They took off all the sheep, mules, and cows; killed all the hogs; caught all the chickens, ducks and geese; and shot the turkeys and tied them to their saddles as they left. The gin-house made the biggest blaze I ever has seen. There was short rations for all the white folks and niggers after that day.

MACK TAYLOR

Near Ridgeway, Fairfield County, SC. Age 97.

I remembers the Yankees. Not many of them come to Miss Margaret's place. Them that did, took pity on her and did nothing but eat, feed their horses, and gallop away.

DELIA THOMPSON

Winnsboro, Fairfield County, SC. Age 88.

Yankees that come to our house was gentleman, they never took a thing, but left provisions for our women folks from their commissary.

MANDA WALKER

Winnsboro, Fairfield County, SC. Age 80.

Wheeler's men was just as hard and wolfish as the Yankees. They say the Yankees was close behind them and they just as well take things as to leave all for the Yankees. Expect that was true, for the Yankees come next day and took the rest of the hog meat, flour, and cows. Had us to run down and catch the chickens for them. They search the house for money, watches, rings, and silverware. Took everything they found, but they didn't set the house afire. There was just about five of them prowling around away from the main army, a foraging, they say.

NANCY WASHINGTON

Marion, Marion County, SC. Age 100.

I was just a girl when the Yankees come through there. They look just like a big blue cloud coming down that road and we children was scared of them. That land round about there was full of them Yankees marching and going on. They never bother my white folks but in some of the places they just ruined everything. Burnt up and tore down all about there.

TENA WHITE

Mt. Pleasant, Charleston County, SC. Age 90.

When the Yankee come through we been at Remley Point. My Ma took care of me. She shut me up and she guard me. The Yankee been go in the colored people house, and they mix all up, and they do just what they want. They been brutish...The beautiful tureen stand so high and have foot so long" lifting her hands, "an all the beautiful thing smash up, and all the meat an ham in the smoke house the distribute them all out to the people, and the dairy broke up, and the horse and the cow kill. Nothing leave. Scatter everything. Nothing leave.

JESSE WILLIAMS

Chester, Chester County, SC. Age 83.

The Yankees didn't come as far up as Chester. They branched off down about Blackstock, took the sunrise side of that place and march on across Catawba River, at Rocky Mount.

MARY WILLIAMS (*VIA* INTERVIEWER F.S. DuPre)

Spartanburg, Spartanburg County, SC. Age Unknown.

She remembered when the Yankee soldiers came into Spartanburg. She said they took all they could get, stole something to eat, just went into the stores and took liquor and handed it out drink by drink to the other soldiers.

GENIA WOODBERRY

Brittons Neck, Marion County, SC. Age 89.

I remember when them Yankees come about there too. Hear Master Jim Stevenson say they must hurry and hide they valuables because the Yankees was coming through there and sweep them out. They bury they silver and they gold watch in the graveyard up in the Beech Field. (The Beech Field was the place where the Indian used to camp long time ago because the peoples used to find all kind of bead and arrow head what they left there.) Then Miss Susan put trunk full of her nice thing to the colored peoples house. Ain't been afraid the Yankees bother them there. Didn't no Yankees come no where about there until after freedom.

JULIA WOODBERRY

Marion, Marion County, SC. Age 70.

They tell me old Sherman didn't come through this section of the country, but he sent somebody to divide out the things like so much corn and so much meat to the colored people. Now, I talking about that what I hear the old people say. Put everything in Ben Thompson hand to deal out the colored people share to them. Yes, ma'am, he was the one had the chair. Talk about Sherman give Ben Thompson the chair, saying what I hear the old people say.

MARY WOODWARD

Winnsboro, Fairfield County, SC. Age 83.

When the Yankees come, I was a sitting in the swing in the front yard. They ride right up and say: 'Where your mistress?' I say: 'I don't know.' They say: 'You is lying. Give her a few lashes and us will find out.' Another say: 'No, us come to free niggers, not to whip them.' Then they ask me for to tell them where the best things was hid. I say: 'I don't know sir.' Then they ransack the house, bust open the smoke house, take the meat, hams, shoulders, molasses barrel, sugar, and meal, put them in a four-horse wagon, set the house, gin-house and barn afire and go on toward Rocky Mount... I forgot to tell you that when the Yankees come and find me a sitting in that swing, I had on a string of beads that Miss Nellie give to me. Them rascals took my beads off my neck, and what you reckon they did with them? Well, if you doesn't know, I does. The scamps, that is one of them did, took my lovely beads and put them around his horse's neck and ride off with them, leaving me sobbing my life out in that swing. They say you must love your enemies and pray for them that despitefully use you but, I never have pray for that Yankee scamp to this day. Although I is Scotch Irish African Associate Reform Presbyterian, the spirit have never moved me to pray for the horse and rider that went off with my beads that my mistress give me. When I tell Master William Woodward, my husband's old master, about it, him say: 'The low dirty skunk, the Lord will take vengeance on him.

DAPHNEY WRIGHT

Scotia, Hampton County, SC. Age 106.

I been right here when the Yankees come through. I been in my house a sitting before the fire, just like I is now. One of them come up and say, 'You know who I is?' I say, 'No.' He say, 'Well, I is come to set you free. You can stay with your old owners if you wants to, but they'll pay you wages.' But they sure did plenty of mischief while they was here. Didn't burn all the houses. Pick out the big handsome house to burn. Burn down Mr. Bill Lawton' house. Mr. Asbury Lawton had a fine house. They burn that. (He Master Tom Lawton's brother.) Burn Mr. Maner's house. Some had put a poor white woman in the house to keep the place; but it didn't make no difference. The soldiers say, This rich house don't belong to you. We going to burn this house!' They'd go through the house and take everything'. Take anything they could find. Take from the white, and take from the colored, too. Take everything out the house! They take from my house. Take something to eat. But I didn't have anything much in my house. Had a little pork and a week's supply of rations... The white folks would bury the silver. But they couldn't always find it again.

BILL YOUNG (*VIA* INTERVIEWER F.S. DuPRE)

Spartanburg, Spartanburg County, SC. Age 83.

He said some Yankee soldiers came by the house at times, but they never bothered anybody on the place. "Of course they would take something to eat, but they never bothered anybody.

BOB YOUNG

Jonesville, Union County, SC Age 75.

War was raging all around Charleston and Columbia when I come in this world so they says, Yankees camped in half mile of Santuc. I is heard that everybody was scared. Has even heard that I cried when them Yankees come, but all I knows is just what I heard... Aunt Phyllis Jeter below when them Yankees got to Santuc, she was a weaving just as hard as she could for her white folks. She say that she started to run, but them Yankees come in the house and throwed away her yarn and took her and tied her to a tree. When she hollered, they whipped her. She say that they was drunk, but they never burnt up nothing in the house. They went on singing, and she got me to playing and got up the yarn from the dirt in the yard and cleaned it. The Yankees never bothered us no more, and they never stayed in Santuc long.

About the Author

PAUL C. GRAHAM holds a Bachelor and Masters Degree in Philosophy from the University of South Carolina. He is past president of the South Carolina Masonic Research Society and the current editor of The Palmetto Partisan, the official journal of the South Carolina Division of the Sons of Confederate Veterans. His writings have appeared in several publications including the Simms Review, the Palmetto Partisan, the Transactions of the SC Masonic Research Society, and the Abbeville Institute's Blog and Review.

In addition to his primary career in the public sector, Mr. Graham has been an adjunct philosophy instructor at Midlands Technical College for over a decade. He is a member of the Society of Independent Southern Historians, the William Gilmore Simms Society, and is co-founder of Shotwell Publishing, LLC. He lives in Cayce, South Carolina, with his beautiful bride, Suzette, their dog, Miss Bella, and two cats, Sully and Mr. Jinx.

You can contact the author *via* his web site:
www.paulcgraham.com

FORTHCOMING TITLES

The Republicans: Annals of the Stupid Party by Clyde N. Wilson

Deliver Us from Evil: The Sack and Destruction of Ursuline Convent, Columbia, S.C. (Voices from the Dust Series) Edited & introduced by Paul C. Graham

Southern Essays by Franklin Sanders

California Confederates by Peter Hefner

And Much, Much More!

O N E L A S T T H I N G

IF YOU ENJOYED THIS BOOK or found it useful, interesting, or informative, we'd be very grateful if you'd post a brief review of it on Amazon.com.

In the current political and cultural climate, it is important that we get accurate, Southern friendly material into the hands of our friends and neighbours. Your support really can make a difference in helping us unapologetically celebrate and defend our Southern heritage and home!

We can be found online at

WWW.SHOTWELLPUBLISHING.COM

THANK YOU FOR YOUR SUPPORT!

68328734R00044

Made in the USA
Lexington, KY
08 October 2017